Table of Contents

INTRODUCTION 2
1   WHAT ARE JOB PORTALS? 3
  1.1   UNDERSTANDING JOB PORTALS 3
  1.2   IMPORTANCE OF JOB PORTALS FOR GOVERNMENT
  AGENCIES 4
  1.3   OVERVIEW OF THE PROJECT LIFECYCLE.....................5
2   RESEARCH AND ANALYSIS 6
  2.1   IDENTIFYING STAKEHOLDER NEEDS............................6
  2.2   MARKET RESEARCH AND COMPETITOR ANALYSIS..........7
  2.3   DEFINING TARGET USER PERSONAS............................8
3   PLANNING THE JOB PORTAL 10
  3.1   SETTING OBJECTIVES AND GOALS 10
  3.2   DEVELOPING A PROJECT TIMELINE............................11
  3.3   BUDGETING AND RESOURCE ALLOCATION 12
4   DESIGNING THE USER EXPERIENCE 13
  4.1   USER INTERFACE (UI) DESIGN PRINCIPLES................13
  4.2   USER EXPERIENCE (UX) CONSIDERATIONS 15
  4.3   ACCESSIBILITY AND COMPLIANCE STANDARDS 16
5   TECHNICAL DEVELOPMENT 17
  5.1   CHOOSING THE RIGHT TECHNOLOGY STACK................17
  5.2   DATABASE DESIGN AND MANAGEMENT........................18
  5.3   INTEGRATING JOB LISTING FEATURES 19
6   SECURITY AND PRIVACY 20
  6.1   UNDERSTANDING DATA PROTECTION REGULATIONS..........20
  6.2   IMPLEMENTING SECURITY PROTOCOLS........................21
  6.3   ENSURING USER PRIVACY 23
7   TESTING AND QUALITY ASSURANCE......................................24
  7.1   DEVELOPING A TESTING STRATEGY 24
  7.2   USER ACCEPTANCE TESTING (UAT)............................25
  7.3   BUG TRACKING AND RESOLUTION...............................26
8   LAUNCHING THE JOB PORTAL 27
  8.1   PREPARING FOR LAUNCH 27
  8.2   MARKETING STRATEGIES FOR PUBLIC AWARENESS..........28
  8.3   MONITORING INITIAL FEEDBACK 29
9   POST-LAUNCH SUPPORT AND MAINTENANCE 31
  9.1   ESTABLISHING SUPPORT CHANNELS 31
  9.2   REGULAR MAINTENANCE AND UPDATES........................32
  9.3   GATHERING USER FEEDBACK FOR IMPROVEMENTS............33
10 MEASURING SUCCESS 34
  10.1 KEY PERFORMANCE INDICATORS (KPIS)........................34
  10.2 ANALYZING USER ENGAGEMENT 35
  10.3 REPORTING AND CONTINUOUS IMPROVEMENT 36
11 CASE STUDIES AND BEST PRACTICES.................................38
  11.1 SUCCESSFUL JOB PORTALS IN GOVERNMENT 38

11.2   LESSONS LEARNED FROM FAILED PROJECTS 39
11.3   BEST PRACTICES FOR FUTURE PROJECTS..............................40
12 CONCLUSION AND FUTURE TRENDS 41
12.1   RECAP OF KEY TAKEAWAYS 41
12.2   THE FUTURE OF JOB PORTALS IN GOVERNMENT 42
12.3   FINAL THOUGHTS AND NEXT STEPS 44

Introduction

Welcome to our *Handy Guides Collection* - a series of publications by Musab Qureshi; he shares researched and proven best practice in an easy-to-understand and focused way. The *Handy Guides Collection* are characterized as per the below:

- Presented in a concise, easy-to-read manner
- Developed using industry standard, proven best practice
- Providing wide covering all of the popular topics our readers need the most
- Typically around 15,000 words
- Mostly text based content with minimal use of images
- Cover the respective subject in a holistic manner – ensuring all/most important detail is covered
- With time will also be available as audio books, on screen flip books and on screen text

Musab (a management consultant from the United Kingdom); may be contacted via email on mail@musab.co.uk – his expertise is sought by smart organizations from across the world. His work profile overview may be seen at https://bit.ly/MusabWorkProfile.

1 What are Job Portals?

1.1 Understanding Job Portals

Understanding job portals is crucial for consultants tasked with building an effective platform for government agencies. A job portal serves as an online space where job seekers and employers connect, streamlining the recruitment process. For government organizations, which often have specific hiring requirements and regulations, a well-designed job portal can enhance transparency, accessibility, and efficiency. This digital solution not only simplifies the application process for candidates but also allows agencies to manage their recruitment needs effectively.

The core functionality of a job portal typically includes job listings, application tracking, and user profiles for both job seekers and employers. In the context of government agencies, compliance with public sector hiring policies is essential. Job portals should be designed to accommodate different hiring protocols, such as civil service rules and equal opportunity employment standards. Features like automated notifications, application status updates, and reporting tools are vital for maintaining compliance and ensuring a smooth recruitment process.

User experience plays a significant role in the success of a job portal. Job seekers should find it easy to navigate the site, search for relevant positions, and submit applications. Incorporating user-friendly interfaces, intuitive search functionalities, and mobile compatibility can significantly enhance engagement. Additionally, providing resources such as resume-building tools, interview tips, and career guidance can further support candidates, making the portal a comprehensive resource for job seekers.

For government agencies, security and data privacy are paramount concerns. A job portal must adhere to strict regulations regarding the handling of personal information and ensure data protection measures are in place. Implementing robust security protocols, including encryption and secure user authentication, is essential to build trust with users. Consultants should also consider how the portal will integrate with existing systems within the agency, ensuring a seamless flow of information while maintaining security standards.

To measure the effectiveness of a job portal, consultants should establish key performance indicators (KPIs) such as user engagement metrics, application completion rates, and time-to-hire statistics. Regularly analyzing these metrics can provide valuable insights into the portal's performance and highlight areas for improvement. By continuously refining the platform based on user feedback and performance data, consultants can ensure that the job portal remains a vital tool for government agencies, facilitating efficient and transparent hiring processes.

1.2 Importance of Job Portals for Government Agencies

Job portals have become an essential tool for government agencies seeking to streamline their recruitment processes and enhance their outreach to potential candidates. In an era where technology plays a pivotal role in virtually every sector, it is imperative for government agencies to adopt digital solutions that facilitate efficient hiring practices. A well-structured job portal not only simplifies the application process for job seekers but also allows agencies to manage job postings, track applications, and evaluate candidate qualifications more effectively.

One of the primary advantages of job portals for government agencies is the ability to reach a wider audience. Traditional recruitment methods, such as print advertisements or community bulletins, often limit the pool of candidates to those who are already familiar with the agency or its mission. In contrast, a job portal can attract a diverse range of applicants from various backgrounds, skills, and experiences. This increased visibility is crucial for building a workforce that reflects the community served by the agency, thereby promoting inclusivity and diversity in hiring practices.

Moreover, job portals enhance the efficiency of the recruitment process. By automating various aspects of hiring, such as application collection, screening, and scheduling interviews, agencies can significantly reduce the time and resources spent on manual recruitment activities. Features like automated notifications and applicant tracking systems can help hiring managers stay organized and informed throughout the selection process. This efficiency not only accelerates hiring timelines but also improves the overall experience for both applicants and agency personnel.

Data analytics is another critical aspect that job portals bring to government agencies. By leveraging data collected through the portal, agencies can gain insights into their recruitment strategies, such as which job postings attract the most applicants or how long it takes to fill certain positions. This information can inform future hiring decisions and strategies, allowing agencies to continuously improve their recruitment processes based on real-time feedback and trends. Additionally, this data-driven approach can help ensure compliance with hiring regulations and policies.

Lastly, job portals can enhance the employer brand of government agencies. A user-friendly, accessible, and informative portal can create a positive impression on job seekers, showcasing the agency's commitment to transparency and engagement. This is particularly important in a competitive job market, where attracting top talent requires a strong employer value proposition. By investing in a robust job portal, government agencies not only optimize their recruitment efforts but also position themselves as desirable employers that value innovation and candidate experience.

1.3 Overview of the Project Lifecycle

The project lifecycle for building a job portal for government agencies consists of several distinct phases that guide the project from conception through to completion. Each phase plays a crucial role in ensuring that the final product meets the needs of both the agency and its users. Understanding this lifecycle is essential for consultants involved in the design and implementation of such portals, as it allows for effective planning, execution, and evaluation. The core phases typically include initiation, planning, execution, monitoring and controlling, and closure.

During the initiation phase, the project is defined at a high level. This stage involves identifying the stakeholders, understanding their needs, and establishing the project's feasibility. Consultants must engage with government representatives to gather requirements and insights about the specific functionalities needed in the job portal. This phase also includes the creation of a project charter, which outlines the project's objectives, scope, and key deliverables. A well-defined initiation phase sets a solid foundation for the subsequent stages of the project lifecycle.

The planning phase is where the groundwork for the entire project is laid. Detailed project plans are developed, including timelines, resource allocation, and budget estimates. Consultants play a vital role in identifying potential risks and creating mitigation strategies. This phase should also encompass the design of the user experience and interface, ensuring that the portal is user-friendly and accessible to diverse populations. By thoroughly planning this phase, consultants can help ensure that the project remains on track and within budget throughout its execution.

Execution is the phase where the actual development of the job portal takes place. This involves coding, testing, and deploying the portal's functionalities. During this stage, effective communication among team members and stakeholders is crucial. Consultants need to facilitate regular check-ins and updates to ensure that the project is progressing according to the established plan. Collaboration with technical teams, designers, and government stakeholders is essential to address any issues that arise promptly and to maintain alignment with the initial vision.

Monitoring and controlling occur concurrently with execution and involve tracking the project's progress against its goals. This phase allows consultants to assess performance metrics, manage changes, and ensure that the project stays aligned with its objectives. Regular reporting and feedback loops are vital to addressing any deviations from the plan. Finally, the closure phase signifies the end of the project lifecycle. This involves finalizing all project activities, conducting post-implementation reviews, and documenting lessons learned. Consultants must ensure that all project deliverables are met and that the job portal is fully operational before transitioning it to the government agency for ongoing maintenance and support.

2 Research and Analysis

2.1 Identifying Stakeholder Needs

Identifying stakeholder needs is a crucial first step in the development of a job portal for government agencies. Stakeholders encompass a broad range of individuals and groups, including government officials, job seekers, employers, and IT personnel. Each of these stakeholders has distinct requirements that must be understood and considered throughout the project lifecycle. Engaging with stakeholders early on helps to ensure that the portal is designed with their needs in mind, ultimately leading to a more effective and user-friendly platform.

To commence the identification process, it is essential to conduct a comprehensive stakeholder analysis. This involves mapping out all potential stakeholders and categorizing them based on their influence and interest in the project. Government officials may prioritize compliance with regulations and ease of use for citizens, while job seekers might emphasize accessibility and the ability to find relevant job listings easily. Employers, on the other hand, will likely focus on the efficiency of the application process and the quality of candidates. This analysis serves as a foundation for further engagement and dialogue.

Once stakeholders are identified, the next step is to gather detailed information on their specific needs and expectations. This can be achieved through various methods, including surveys, interviews, and focus groups. These interactions provide valuable insights into what stakeholders envision for the job portal. For example, job seekers may express the need for mobile accessibility and user-friendly navigation, while employers may request advanced filtering options for job postings. Collecting qualitative and quantitative data during this phase ensures that the project team has a well-rounded understanding of stakeholder perspectives.

It is also important to recognize that stakeholder needs may evolve over time. As the project progresses, continuous engagement is necessary to reassess these requirements. Regular check-ins and feedback sessions can help identify any changes in priorities or emerging needs that may not have been initially apparent. This iterative approach allows the project team to remain agile and responsive, ultimately leading to a portal that better serves all stakeholders involved.

In conclusion, identifying stakeholder needs is an ongoing process that lays the groundwork for a successful job portal tailored to the specific context of government agencies. By conducting thorough analyses, employing effective data-gathering techniques, and maintaining open lines of communication, consultants can ensure that the final product not only meets but exceeds the expectations of its users. A well-defined understanding of stakeholder needs is essential for creating a job portal that enhances the employment landscape and fosters effective connections between job seekers and employers.

2.2 Market Research and Competitor Analysis

Market research and competitor analysis are crucial steps in developing a job portal for government agencies. Understanding the landscape in which the portal will operate allows consultants to identify the needs of the target audience, which primarily includes job seekers, government employers, and other stakeholders. This research should begin with an in-depth analysis of the existing job portals, both within the public sector and the broader job market. By examining the features, user interfaces, and service offerings of competitors, consultants can pinpoint gaps in the market and opportunities for differentiation. This analysis should also consider user reviews and feedback to understand what works well and what does not, providing insights into user expectations.

It is essential to segment the target market to tailor the job portal effectively. Government job seekers vary in demographics, experiences, and preferences. Conducting surveys, focus groups, and interviews can help gather qualitative data on what features users find most valuable, such as job alerts, application tracking, or resources for navigating the hiring process.

Additionally, understanding the needs of government agencies that will utilize the portal is equally important. This includes their requirements for compliance, reporting, and integration with existing human resource systems. A well-rounded market research strategy will ensure that the portal meets the diverse needs of all stakeholders involved.

Competitor analysis should not only focus on direct competitors but also on indirect ones that provide similar services. By evaluating platforms that cater to private sector job seekers or niche employment services, consultants can glean valuable insights into innovative features and user engagement strategies. It is important to analyze competitors' marketing strategies as well, including their outreach methods, branding, and user acquisition tactics. This understanding can inform the development of a robust marketing plan that effectively communicates the unique value proposition of the government job portal.

Additionally, the regulatory environment surrounding government employment must be considered during this phase. Various laws and regulations govern the hiring processes in public agencies, and understanding these legal requirements is critical to the portal's design and functionality. Competitors that have successfully navigated these regulations can serve as case studies for best practices. Consultants should also keep an eye on emerging trends in the job market, such as the increasing use of artificial intelligence in recruitment, to ensure the portal remains relevant and competitive in a rapidly evolving landscape.

Finally, synthesizing the findings from market research and competitor analysis will create a solid foundation for the portal's development. Consultants should create detailed personas that represent the primary users of the job portal, enabling them to design features that cater specifically to these personas. Furthermore, the insights gained should inform decisions about technology stacks, user experience design, and marketing strategies. By prioritizing user needs and maintaining a keen awareness of the competitive landscape, consultants can develop a job portal that not only meets regulatory requirements but also enhances the overall job-seeking experience for government employment.

2.3 Defining Target User Personas

Defining target user personas is a crucial step in the development of a job portal for government agencies. User personas represent the different segments of the audience that will interact with the portal, including job seekers, employers, and government officials. Each persona embodies specific characteristics, needs, and behaviors that must be understood to create an effective and user-friendly platform. By defining these personas, consultants can ensure that the job portal meets the diverse requirements of its users, thereby enhancing overall engagement and satisfaction.

To begin, consultants should conduct thorough research to gather data on potential users. This can include surveys, interviews, and focus groups with job seekers, hiring managers, and other stakeholders within government organizations. It is important to gather demographic information, such as age, education level, and career aspirations, as well as insights into user motivations and pain points. For example, job seekers may prioritize ease of application and access to resources, while employers may focus on the quality of candidates and the efficiency of the hiring process. By compiling this data, consultants can create detailed profiles that represent the various user types.

Once the research is complete, consultants can identify key traits and behaviors that define each persona. This includes understanding their goals, challenges, and preferred methods of communication. For instance, a job seeker persona may include a recent college graduate looking for entry-level positions, whereas another persona may represent a seasoned professional seeking career advancement. By clearly outlining these aspects, consultants can tailor the job portal's features and content to align with the unique needs of each user group, ensuring a more personalized experience.

In addition to user characteristics, consultants should consider the context in which users will engage with the job portal. This includes the devices they will use, their level of technological proficiency, and the environments in which they are accessing the platform. For example, younger job seekers may primarily use mobile devices, while older users might prefer desktop access. Recognizing these differences can inform the design and functionality of the portal, making it more accessible and user-friendly for all personas.

Finally, the defined user personas should be revisited and refined throughout the development process. As the project progresses and feedback is gathered, consultants should remain flexible in adapting the personas to reflect new insights and changing user needs. This iterative approach not only enhances the job portal's effectiveness but also fosters a stronger connection between the platform and its users. By continually aligning the portal's offerings with the evolving expectations of its target audience, consultants can help ensure the success and longevity of the job portal for government agencies.

3 Planning the Job Portal

3.1 Setting Objectives and Goals

Setting objectives and goals is a critical first step in the development of a job portal for government agencies. These objectives serve as the foundation upon which the project will be built, guiding the planning, execution, and evaluation phases. The primary objective should focus on meeting the specific needs of government organizations, such as increasing accessibility, improving efficiency in the recruitment process, and ensuring compliance with legal and regulatory requirements. Establishing clear objectives helps align the project with the strategic goals of the agency, ensuring that the job portal serves its intended purpose effectively.

When defining objectives, it is essential to consider both the short-term and long-term goals of the project. Short-term goals may include launching a minimum viable product (MVP) that allows agencies to test functionalities and gather feedback. Long-term goals should encompass broader aspirations such as creating a user-friendly platform that integrates seamlessly with existing government systems, facilitates collaboration among agencies, and enhances the job search experience for potential candidates. By balancing these goals, consultants can ensure that the portal evolves to meet changing needs over time.

Measurable key performance indicators (KPIs) should accompany each objective to track progress and evaluate success. These KPIs could include metrics such as the number of job postings created, user engagement levels, application completion rates, and the time taken to fill positions. Establishing specific benchmarks will provide insights into the portal's effectiveness and highlight areas for improvement. Regular assessment against these KPIs enables consultants to make data-driven decisions and adapt strategies to enhance the portal continually.

Collaboration with stakeholders is another crucial aspect of setting objectives and goals. Engaging with government agencies, hiring managers, and potential job seekers allows consultants to gather diverse perspectives and insights. This collaborative approach can lead to the identification of critical features and functionalities that may not have been initially considered. Furthermore, involving stakeholders in the goal-setting process fosters ownership and commitment to the project, increasing the likelihood of successful implementation and adoption.

Lastly, it is important to remain adaptable throughout the project lifecycle. As technology and job market dynamics evolve, the objectives and goals may need to be revisited and refined. Consultants should establish a review process to evaluate the relevance and effectiveness of the goals periodically. This flexibility ensures that the job portal remains aligned with the strategic direction of the government agency and continues to meet the needs of its users, ultimately contributing to a more efficient and effective recruitment process.

3.2 Developing a Project Timeline

Developing a project timeline is a critical step in the successful creation of a job portal for government agencies. A well-structured timeline serves as a roadmap that outlines the various phases of the project, ensuring that all stakeholders are aligned and aware of their responsibilities. It involves breaking down the entire project into manageable tasks, assigning deadlines, and establishing clear milestones that allow for tracking progress. By developing an effective timeline, consultants can mitigate risks, streamline workflows, and enhance communication among team members.

The first step in creating a project timeline is to identify the key phases of the project. Typically, these phases include project initiation, planning, execution, monitoring, and closure. During the initiation phase, consultants must gather requirements, define the project scope, and identify stakeholders. Planning involves developing a detailed project plan that outlines tasks, roles, and resources. Execution is where the actual development of the job portal occurs, while monitoring ensures that progress aligns with the established timeline. Finally, the closure phase focuses on project evaluation and the delivery of the final product.

Once the phases are established, the next task is to break down each phase into specific tasks and subtasks. This granular approach allows for a clearer understanding of what needs to be accomplished at each stage. For example, in the planning phase, tasks may include conducting user research, designing the portal architecture, and developing a content strategy. Each task should be assigned a realistic timeline based on its complexity and interdependencies with other tasks. This detailed breakdown promotes accountability and helps consultants manage their time effectively.

Additionally, incorporating milestones into the project timeline is essential for measuring progress and maintaining motivation. Milestones act as checkpoints that signify the completion of significant phases or deliverables. For instance, reaching the prototype stage of the job portal can be marked as a milestone that allows for stakeholder review and feedback. Setting these milestones not only helps in tracking progress but also provides opportunities to assess whether the project is on track or if adjustments need to be made to the timeline.

Lastly, it is vital to remain flexible and adaptable throughout the project timeline. Unforeseen challenges and changes in requirements may arise, particularly in a government context where regulations and stakeholder needs can shift. Consultants must build in buffer time for each phase and be prepared to revisit and revise the timeline as necessary. Regular meetings with the team and stakeholders can facilitate open communication, allowing for timely adjustments and ensuring that the project remains aligned with its objectives. By adopting a proactive approach to timeline management, consultants can enhance the likelihood of delivering a successful job portal for government agencies.

3.3 Budgeting and Resource Allocation

Budgeting and resource allocation are critical elements in the successful development of a job portal for government agencies. Creating an effective budget requires a thorough understanding of the project's scope, including the technological requirements, staffing needs, and ongoing operational costs. Consultants must begin by conducting a needs assessment to identify the specific functionalities and features that the portal will offer. This assessment will guide the allocation of financial resources, ensuring that funds are directed toward the most essential components of the project, such as user interface design, database management, and security protocols.

Once the needs assessment is complete, consultants should develop a detailed budget that outlines all projected expenses. This budget should include initial development costs, such as software licenses, server hosting, and hiring skilled personnel, as well as ongoing costs like maintenance, updates, and customer support. It is crucial to account for unexpected expenses by including a contingency fund, typically around 10-15% of the total budget. This financial foresight helps mitigate risks associated with project delays or unforeseen technical challenges that may arise during the portal's development and operation.

Resource allocation is equally important, as it involves the strategic distribution of both financial and human resources. Consultants must identify the key stakeholders and team members who will contribute to the project, assigning roles based on expertise and availability. This may include developers, designers, project managers, and subject matter experts. Clear communication and collaboration among team members are essential to ensure that resources are utilized efficiently and that everyone is aligned with the project's goals and timelines.

In the context of government agencies, it is also vital to consider compliance and regulatory requirements when budgeting and allocating resources. Consultants should familiarize themselves with relevant laws and guidelines related to public sector projects, which may impose specific constraints on spending and resource use. Adhering to these regulations not only ensures legal compliance but also builds trust with stakeholders and the public, fostering transparency in how taxpayer dollars are utilized in the development of the job portal.

Finally, ongoing evaluation of the budget and resource allocation throughout the project lifecycle is necessary to ensure that the job portal remains aligned with its objectives. Regular financial reviews and performance assessments can help identify areas where adjustments may be needed, whether it's reallocating funds to address emerging needs or scaling back in areas that are underperforming. By maintaining a flexible approach to budgeting and resource allocation, consultants can adapt to changes in project requirements and ensure the successful delivery of a robust job portal that meets the needs of government agencies and their constituents.

4 Designing the User Experience

4.1 User Interface (UI) Design Principles

User Interface (UI) design principles are vital in creating an effective job portal for government agencies. A user-friendly interface ensures that job seekers, employers, and agency staff can navigate the platform with ease, promoting higher engagement and satisfaction. At the foundation of UI design are several key principles, including consistency, simplicity, feedback, accessibility, and aesthetics. Understanding and implementing these principles can significantly enhance the usability and functionality of the job portal.

Consistency is crucial in UI design, as it establishes a cohesive look and feel across the platform. This principle ensures that elements such as buttons, fonts, colors, and layouts remain uniform throughout the site. By maintaining consistency, users become familiar with the interface quickly, reducing the learning curve. For a government job portal, it is essential that users can easily recognize and understand the various features without confusion. For instance, if job listings are displayed in a particular format on one page, the same format should be used across all listings to provide a seamless experience.

Simplicity in design cannot be overstated. The job portal should prioritize essential functions, allowing users to complete tasks without unnecessary distractions. This principle involves minimizing clutter and focusing on the core features that users need, such as job search filters, application submission, and notification settings. A simplified design not only enhances user experience but also decreases the likelihood of user errors. Government job portals should cater to a diverse audience, including individuals with varying levels of technical proficiency, making simplicity an essential aspect of the design process.

Feedback is another critical principle in UI design. It is important to provide users with immediate and clear responses to their actions on the job portal. For example, when a user submits an application, they should receive a confirmation message indicating successful submission. This feedback reassures users that their actions have been recognized and helps to reinforce their engagement with the portal. Additionally, feedback can include error messages that guide users on how to correct mistakes, further improving the overall user experience.

Accessibility must be at the forefront of UI design for government job portals. The platform should be designed to accommodate users with disabilities, ensuring compliance with standards such as the Web Content Accessibility Guidelines (WCAG). This includes providing alternative text for images, ensuring sufficient color contrast, and enabling keyboard navigation. By prioritizing accessibility, the job portal can reach a broader audience, ensuring that all individuals, regardless of their abilities, have equal access to job opportunities.

Finally, aesthetics play a significant role in UI design, impacting users' first impressions and overall satisfaction with the job portal. A visually appealing design can create a sense of trust and professionalism, which is especially important for government agencies. The choice of colors, typography, and imagery should align with the agency's branding while also promoting readability and ease of use. However, it is crucial to strike a balance between aesthetic appeal and functionality, ensuring that the design enhances, rather than detracts from, the user experience. By following these UI design principles, consultants can create a job portal that effectively meets the needs of government agencies and their diverse user base.

4.2 User Experience (UX) Considerations

User experience (UX) is a critical component in the development of a job portal for government agencies, as it directly influences user satisfaction and engagement. For consultants working on such projects, understanding the needs and preferences of diverse user groups—such as job seekers, employers, and government personnel—is paramount. A well-designed UX not only facilitates ease of use but also enhances accessibility, making it essential for the job portal to cater to all potential users, including those with disabilities.

To achieve an optimal UX, it is vital to conduct thorough user research at the outset of the project. This includes surveys, interviews, and usability testing with real users to gather insights into their expectations and pain points. Understanding the specific demographics of users, including age, tech-savviness, and familiarity with government processes, will inform design decisions. For instance, a user-friendly interface that simplifies navigation and minimizes the cognitive load will be beneficial for individuals who may not be as comfortable with technology.

Designing an intuitive user journey is another critical consideration. The job portal should guide users seamlessly from one step to the next, whether they are searching for job listings or submitting applications. This can be achieved through clear visual hierarchy, consistent layout, and logical pathways that break down complex tasks into manageable steps. Incorporating features such as predictive search, filtering options, and easily accessible FAQs will enhance the overall experience, allowing users to find relevant information quickly and efficiently.

Accessibility is also a cornerstone of effective UX design in job portals for government agencies. Compliance with accessibility standards, such as the Web Content Accessibility Guidelines (WCAG), ensures that the portal is usable for individuals with disabilities. This includes providing alternative text for images, ensuring keyboard navigability, and using high-contrast color schemes for readability. By prioritizing accessibility, consultants can create a job portal that is inclusive, allowing all users to benefit from the platform's offerings.

Finally, ongoing evaluation and iteration of the UX are essential for long-term success. After the initial launch, consultants should establish metrics to assess user engagement and satisfaction, such as bounce rates, time on page, and user feedback. Regularly updating the portal based on user input and technological advancements will help maintain its relevance and effectiveness. By fostering a continuous improvement mindset, consultants can ensure that the job portal not only meets current needs but also adapts to future changes in user expectations and government policies.

4.3 Accessibility and Compliance Standards

Accessibility and compliance standards are critical components in the development of job portals for government agencies. These standards ensure that the portal is usable by all individuals, including those with disabilities, and adheres to legal regulations. The primary frameworks guiding these requirements include the Web Content Accessibility Guidelines (WCAG) and the Americans with Disabilities Act (ADA). Consultants should prioritize these guidelines during the planning and design phases to create an inclusive environment that caters to a diverse user base.

One of the key aspects of accessibility is ensuring that the job portal can be navigated and understood by individuals with varying abilities. This includes providing alternative text for images, ensuring keyboard navigability, and designing forms that are easy to complete. Additionally, color contrast must be considered to aid users with visual impairments. By integrating these elements from the outset, consultants can significantly enhance the user experience and meet compliance standards that are often mandated by law for government websites.

Compliance standards also involve rigorous testing and validation processes to confirm that the portal meets established guidelines. This includes conducting usability tests with diverse user groups, including individuals with disabilities, to gather feedback and make necessary adjustments. Automated tools can assist in identifying potential accessibility issues, but human testing remains essential to capture the nuances of user experience. Consultants should establish a clear testing protocol to ensure that the portal not only complies with legal requirements but also serves its intended purpose effectively.

Furthermore, consultants must stay informed about changing regulations and best practices in accessibility. Government agencies often update their policies to reflect new standards, and staying compliant requires ongoing education and adaptation. Regular audits of the portal should be conducted to ensure continued adherence to accessibility guidelines. This proactive approach can help mitigate legal risks and reinforce the agency's commitment to inclusivity.

In conclusion, integrating accessibility and compliance standards into the development of a job portal for government agencies is not merely a legal obligation but also a moral imperative. By focusing on user-centered design principles and maintaining a commitment to inclusivity, consultants can create a platform that is not only compliant but also accessible and user-friendly. Such efforts ultimately enhance the effectiveness of the job portal, ensuring that it serves the needs of all users, thereby fostering a more equitable job search experience.

5 Technical Development

5.1 Choosing the Right Technology Stack

Choosing the right technology stack is a critical decision that can significantly impact the success of a job portal for government agencies. A well-considered technology stack not only supports the functional requirements of the platform but also ensures scalability, security, and maintainability. Consultants must evaluate various components, including front-end and back-end technologies, databases, hosting solutions, and third-party integrations. This evaluation should align with the specific requirements of the government agency, including compliance with regulatory standards and the need for accessibility features.

Front-end technologies are crucial for creating an engaging user experience. Popular frameworks like React, Angular, or Vue.js can facilitate the development of dynamic and responsive interfaces. These frameworks enable consultants to build user-friendly portals that cater to a diverse audience, including job seekers and employers. The choice of front-end technology should also consider the familiarity of the development team with these tools, as well as the availability of community support and resources. Prioritizing accessibility in the design ensures that all users, including those with disabilities, can navigate and utilize the portal effectively.

On the back end, the technology stack must provide a robust framework for handling data processing, user authentication, and business logic. Popular choices include Node.js, Python with Django or Flask, and Ruby on Rails. Each of these frameworks has its strengths, such as ease of use, speed of development, and security features. When selecting a back-end technology, consultants should also consider the anticipated user load and data volume. Scalability is essential, especially for government job portals that may experience fluctuating traffic during peak hiring seasons.

Database selection is another vital aspect of the technology stack. Relational databases like PostgreSQL or MySQL are often favored for their reliability and structured query capabilities, while NoSQL databases like MongoDB can be suitable for applications requiring flexibility in data storage. The choice should reflect the nature of the data being managed, whether structured or unstructured, and the need for complex queries. Additionally, consultants should consider factors such as data security, backup solutions, and compliance with government regulations regarding data storage and processing.

Lastly, the hosting solution plays a pivotal role in the performance and reliability of the job portal. Cloud services like Amazon Web Services, Microsoft Azure, or Google Cloud Platform offer scalability and reliability, which are crucial for government applications. These platforms provide various services, including load balancing, content delivery networks, and security features that enhance the portal's resilience. Consultants must also consider ongoing maintenance and support, as well as the costs associated with different hosting options. By carefully assessing these components, consultants can create a comprehensive technology stack that meets the unique needs of government agencies and sets the foundation for a successful job portal.

5.2 Database Design and Management

Database design and management are critical components in the development of a job portal for government agencies. A well-structured database not only ensures efficient data storage and retrieval but also enhances the overall performance of the portal. It is essential to establish a clear understanding of the types of data that will be collected, processed, and stored. This includes job listings, user profiles, application submissions, and administrative records. By categorizing these data types, consultants can design a database schema that reflects the relationships and hierarchies inherent in the dataset, ultimately leading to a more intuitive and functional portal.

When designing the database, consultants should adopt a relational database management system (RDBMS) to facilitate structured query language (SQL) operations. RDBMS offers various advantages such as data integrity, security, and support for complex queries. The database schema should be normalized to eliminate redundancy and ensure that each piece of data is stored only once. For instance, job listings should be linked to specific categories and requirements, while user profiles should be connected to application history and preferences. This approach not only improves data accuracy but also enhances the efficiency of data retrieval processes, which is crucial for user experience.

Data management extends beyond initial design; it involves ongoing maintenance, backup, and optimization practices. Implementing a robust data management strategy is vital for ensuring the longevity of the job portal. Regular backups safeguard against data loss, while optimization techniques, such as indexing, can significantly improve query performance. Additionally, data governance policies should be established to manage data access, ensuring that sensitive information is protected while still allowing authorized users to perform their tasks effectively. This balance is particularly important in government agencies where data privacy and compliance with regulations are paramount.

Analytics plays a significant role in the management of the job portal's database. By integrating analytical tools, consultants can gain insights into user behavior, job trends, and application success rates. This data can inform decision-making processes, helping government agencies to refine job listings, enhance user engagement, and improve overall service delivery. Furthermore, analytics can assist in identifying areas for improvement within the portal, enabling continuous development and adaptation to meet the evolving needs of job seekers and employers alike.

In conclusion, successful database design and management are foundational to building an effective job portal for government organizations. By focusing on a structured approach to data organization, employing a reliable RDBMS, and implementing strong data management practices, consultants can ensure that the portal operates efficiently and effectively. The incorporation of analytics further enhances the portal's capabilities, allowing for informed decision-making and continuous improvement. Ultimately, a well-designed database will not only streamline the job application process but also contribute to the overall success of the government's employment initiatives.

5.3 Integrating Job Listing Features

Integrating job listing features is a crucial aspect of developing a successful job portal for government agencies. These features not only enhance user experience but also streamline the hiring process for both applicants and recruiters. A well-designed job listing interface should include search functionality, filtering options, and detailed job descriptions. By implementing these elements, consultants can ensure that job seekers find relevant opportunities easily, while also allowing employers to reach a wider audience.

The search functionality should be robust and user-friendly. It should enable users to search by keywords, job titles, locations, and other relevant criteria. An advanced search option can further improve user experience by allowing job seekers to narrow down their results based on specific parameters such as job type, salary range, and required qualifications. This feature is essential for government job portals, where applicants may be looking for niche positions that require specialized skills or certifications.

Filtering options are equally important in refining search results. Users should be able to filter job listings by date posted, application deadlines, and organizational departments. This functionality not only saves time for job seekers but also helps them stay organized during their application process.

For government agencies, timely access to new job listings can be a matter of urgency, and effective filtering ensures that applicants do not miss out on opportunities that match their qualifications and interests.

Detailed job descriptions play a vital role in attracting the right candidates. Each listing should include essential information such as job responsibilities, qualifications, application procedures, and contact details of the hiring department. Additionally, incorporating multimedia elements, such as videos or infographics, can provide a more engaging overview of the job and the agency. This approach not only helps candidates understand the position better but also reflects positively on the agency's branding and commitment to transparency.

Lastly, integrating features that allow for easy application submission is essential. A streamlined application process can greatly enhance user satisfaction and increase the number of applications received. This may involve creating an intuitive online application form, allowing for resume uploads, and providing clear instructions on how to apply. By optimizing these job listing features, consultants can contribute to a more efficient hiring process that benefits both job seekers and government agencies, ultimately leading to a successful job portal.

6 Security and Privacy

6.1 Understanding Data Protection Regulations

Understanding data protection regulations is crucial for consultants involved in building job portals for government agencies. These regulations ensure that personal information collected from job seekers is handled responsibly and securely. With the increasing emphasis on data privacy, consultants must be well-versed in the legal landscape to mitigate risks and comply with applicable laws. Key regulations such as the General Data Protection Regulation (GDPR) and the California Consumer Privacy Act (CCPA) set stringent guidelines regarding the collection, storage, and processing of personal data, making it imperative for consultants to integrate these considerations into their project plans.

Data protection regulations serve multiple purposes, such as safeguarding individual privacy, establishing accountability for organizations, and promoting transparency in data handling practices. For government job portals, where sensitive personal information is often processed, understanding these regulations helps in designing systems that protect user data while fulfilling public service goals. Consultants should be aware that non-compliance can lead to significant penalties, reputational damage, and loss of public trust, which underscores the importance of implementing robust data protection measures from the outset.

Consultants must also consider the specific requirements of various data protection laws, as they can differ significantly across jurisdictions. In addition to GDPR and CCPA, regulations like the Health Insurance Portability and Accountability Act (HIPAA) may apply if the portal handles health-related information. Understanding the nuances of these regulations allows consultants to tailor their approaches based on the specific needs of the government agency and the demographic of job seekers. This includes analyzing how data is collected, processed, and shared, as well as ensuring that appropriate consent mechanisms are in place.

Moreover, establishing a culture of data protection within the project team is essential for compliance. This involves training team members on data handling practices and creating clear protocols for managing personal information. Consultants should advocate for regular audits and assessments to identify potential vulnerabilities in the system that could lead to data breaches. By fostering a proactive approach to data protection, consultants can ensure that the job portal not only meets regulatory requirements but also enhances the overall user experience by instilling confidence in data security.

Finally, consultants should stay informed about the evolving landscape of data protection regulations. As technology advances and public concern regarding privacy grows, regulatory frameworks are likely to adapt, necessitating continuous education and adaptation in project management practices. Engaging with legal experts or data protection officers can provide valuable insights into emerging trends and best practices. By prioritizing data protection from the initial stages of development, consultants can build job portals that serve government agencies effectively while upholding the highest standards of data privacy.

6.2 Implementing Security Protocols

Implementing security protocols is a critical aspect of developing a job portal for government agencies. Given the sensitive nature of the information involved, including personal data of applicants and organizational details, it is essential to adopt a comprehensive security framework. This framework must encompass various layers of protection, including network security, application security, and data security. Each layer plays a pivotal role in safeguarding the portal from potential threats, ensuring that both the agency and its users can trust the system.

The first step in implementing security protocols is conducting a thorough risk assessment. This assessment should identify potential vulnerabilities within the portal and evaluate the potential impact of security breaches. Consultants should consider various threat vectors, such as unauthorized access, data breaches, and denial-of-service attacks. By understanding these risks, consultants can prioritize the implementation of security measures that will most effectively mitigate them. Regular audits and updates to the risk assessment should also be part of the ongoing security strategy to adapt to evolving threats.

Once risks have been identified, establishing strong authentication mechanisms is vital. Multi-factor authentication (MFA) should be implemented to ensure that only authorized users can access the portal. This could involve a combination of something the user knows (a password), something the user has (a smartphone app for verification), and something the user is (biometric verification). By reinforcing access control, the portal can significantly reduce the risk of unauthorized access, which is particularly important for government job portals handling confidential information.

Data encryption is another critical component of security protocols. All sensitive information, whether in transit or at rest, should be encrypted using industry-standard protocols. This means that data transmitted between users and the portal, as well as stored data within the system, is rendered unreadable to unauthorized parties. Consultants should ensure that the encryption methods used comply with relevant regulations and standards, such as the General Data Protection Regulation (GDPR) and the Federal Information Security Management Act (FISMA), to provide an additional layer of compliance and security.

Finally, ongoing training and awareness programs for all users of the job portal are essential to maintaining security over time. Employees and users must be educated about common security threats, such as phishing scams and social engineering tactics, and should be trained on best practices for maintaining security. Regular updates and refresher courses can help reinforce the importance of security protocols and ensure that everyone involved in using the portal understands their role in keeping the system secure. By fostering a culture of security awareness, government agencies can enhance their defenses against potential threats, ultimately leading to a more secure and trustworthy job portal.

6.3 Ensuring User Privacy

Ensuring user privacy is a critical component in the development of a job portal for government agencies. As consultants, understanding the intricacies of user data management will not only enhance the portal's credibility but also instill trust among users. Given the sensitive nature of personal information such as resumes, contact details, and employment history, it is essential to implement robust privacy measures throughout the portal's design and functionality. This involves not only adhering to legal standards but also adopting best practices that go beyond compliance.

One of the primary steps in ensuring user privacy is the implementation of strong data encryption protocols. By encrypting data both at rest and in transit, you protect sensitive information from unauthorized access. This means that personal details shared by job seekers will be secure from potential breaches. Additionally, employing secure socket layer (SSL) certificates for website security can further enhance data protection, ensuring a secure connection between the user's browser and the job portal.

Another vital aspect is the establishment of clear data usage policies. Users must be informed about what data is being collected, how it will be used, and with whom it may be shared. Transparency is key; therefore, creating an easily accessible privacy policy that outlines these details fosters trust. This policy should also detail users' rights concerning their data, including the ability to access, modify, or delete their information. By ensuring clear communication of these policies, you help users feel more secure in their interactions with the portal.

Moreover, implementing user authentication mechanisms is crucial for maintaining privacy. Multi-factor authentication (MFA) can significantly reduce the risk of unauthorized access. By requiring additional verification steps, such as a one-time password sent to the user's mobile device, you create an added layer of security. This is particularly important for government agencies, where the integrity of the information is paramount. Robust authentication processes not only protect user data but also enhance the overall security framework of the job portal.

Finally, regular audits and assessments of privacy practices should be part of the ongoing maintenance of the job portal. This includes monitoring for potential vulnerabilities and ensuring compliance with evolving regulations and standards. Engaging in periodic reviews allows for the identification of areas for improvement and the implementation of new privacy technologies as they become available. By committing to continuous improvement in user privacy practices, consultants can ensure that the job portal remains a secure and trusted resource for job seekers engaging with government agencies.

7 Testing and Quality Assurance

7.1 Developing a Testing Strategy

Developing a testing strategy is a critical phase in the creation of a job portal for government agencies, ensuring that the platform meets all functional requirements and user expectations. A comprehensive testing strategy should encompass various testing methodologies, including unit testing, integration testing, system testing, and user acceptance testing. Each of these testing types serves a specific purpose, allowing consultants to identify potential issues early in the development cycle and mitigate risks before the final launch. It is essential to outline the objectives for each testing stage, defining what success looks like and determining the metrics to evaluate performance.

In the context of a job portal, unit testing should focus on individual components of the application. This may include testing the functionality of job postings, user registration, and application submission processes. By isolating these elements, consultants can ensure that each piece functions correctly before integrating them into the larger system. Unit tests should be automated where possible to facilitate rapid feedback, allowing developers to address issues immediately as they arise. This proactive approach helps maintain a high standard of code quality and reliability.

Integration testing follows unit testing and examines how different components of the job portal interact with one another. For instance, it is crucial to test the integration between the user interface and the database to ensure that data flows smoothly and accurately reflects user actions. In this stage, consultants should also evaluate the interactions between third-party services, such as payment gateways or notification systems. Identifying integration issues early can prevent costly fixes later in the development process and contribute to a more seamless user experience.

System testing is the next step, where the entire job portal is evaluated in a simulated environment that closely resembles the production setting. This phase should assess the platform's performance under various scenarios, including high user traffic, to ensure it can handle the expected load. Additionally, system testing should encompass security testing to safeguard sensitive user data and compliance testing to ensure the portal meets all relevant government regulations. By rigorously assessing the system as a whole, consultants can identify any deficiencies that may impede the user experience or violate compliance standards.

Finally, user acceptance testing (UAT) is a vital component of the testing strategy, as it involves real users from the target audience interacting with the job portal. This phase provides valuable insights into usability, accessibility, and overall satisfaction. Consultants should gather feedback from users to identify any issues they encounter and make necessary adjustments before the official launch. UAT is not just about finding bugs; it is also an opportunity to validate that the portal meets the needs of government agencies and their constituents, ensuring that the final product is user-friendly and effective in serving its purpose.

7.2 User Acceptance Testing (UAT)

User Acceptance Testing (UAT) is a critical phase in the development of a job portal for government agencies, serving as the final validation step before the system goes live. This testing process ensures that the portal meets the specified requirements and functions as intended from the end user's perspective. UAT engages real users, typically from the government agency or stakeholders, who interact with the system to identify any issues, verify workflows, and confirm that the portal aligns with their expectations and needs. This stage is essential for mitigating risks and ensuring that the portal can effectively serve its purpose.

The UAT process begins with the establishment of clear objectives and criteria for acceptance. Consultants must work closely with government stakeholders to define what success looks like for the job portal. This includes understanding the end users' needs, the functionalities they require, and the overall user experience they anticipate. Creating comprehensive UAT plans that outline test cases, scenarios, and expected outcomes is crucial. These plans should reflect real-world usage and scenarios that users will encounter as they navigate the portal.

Training and preparation for users involved in UAT is another vital component. It is important to provide participants with adequate training on how to use the portal, including any new features that may have been implemented since the initial design phase. This training ensures that users feel confident in their ability to test the system effectively. Additionally, consultants should communicate the importance of this testing phase and encourage constructive feedback, fostering a collaborative environment where users feel comfortable reporting issues or suggesting improvements.

During UAT, consultants should facilitate the testing sessions, guiding users through the various functionalities of the portal. This includes monitoring user interactions, gathering feedback, and documenting any issues encountered. It's essential to create an open channel for communication, allowing users to express their thoughts on usability, accessibility, and any technical glitches.

This feedback is invaluable, as it provides insight into how well the portal meets the users' needs and identifies areas for improvement before the final launch.

After UAT is complete, the findings must be reviewed and addressed promptly. Consultants should analyze the feedback and prioritize necessary changes or fixes based on user input. This iterative process may require several cycles of testing and refinement before the portal is deemed ready for launch. Ultimately, a successful UAT phase not only assures that the job portal is functional and user-friendly but also enhances the overall satisfaction of stakeholders and end users, paving the way for a successful rollout and adoption of the new system within the government agency.

7.3 Bug Tracking and Resolution

Effective bug tracking and resolution is a critical component in the development of a job portal for government agencies. Given the importance of these platforms in connecting job seekers with public sector opportunities, ensuring a seamless user experience is paramount. The first step in establishing a robust bug tracking system is to choose the right tools tailored for the project's specific needs. Popular options include Jira, Bugzilla, and Trello, each offering unique features that facilitate the identification and management of bugs. These tools not only help in logging issues but also assist in prioritizing them based on their impact on the user experience and the overall functionality of the portal.

Once the bug tracking tool is in place, the next step is to establish a clear reporting process. All team members, including developers, testers, and project managers, should be trained on how to report bugs effectively. This includes providing detailed information such as the steps to reproduce the issue, screenshots, and any relevant system information. A well-defined reporting process ensures that no bugs are overlooked and that they are documented in a manner that makes them easier to resolve. Regular meetings should be scheduled to review reported bugs, allowing the team to prioritize issues that need immediate attention and strategize on resolutions.

The resolution process itself should be systematic and efficient. After identifying a bug, it is essential to assign it to the appropriate team member based on their expertise and workload. This delegation can significantly speed up the resolution process. Additionally, implementing a workflow that includes stages such as 'In Progress,' 'Resolved,' and 'Verified' can help track the status of each bug. Each resolution should be thoroughly tested before being marked as complete, ensuring that the fix does not introduce new issues or adversely affect other functionalities in the job portal.

Communication plays a vital role in bug tracking and resolution. Keeping all stakeholders informed about the status of bug fixes is essential for transparency and trust. Regular updates can be communicated through the bug tracking tool or during team meetings, allowing everyone involved to have a clear understanding of ongoing efforts. Furthermore, feedback from end-users can provide valuable insights into the effectiveness of bug fixes and highlight any lingering issues that may require additional attention.

Finally, it is essential to analyze bug data post-resolution to identify patterns and areas for improvement. By regularly reviewing the types, frequency, and severity of bugs, consultants can gain insights into potential weaknesses in the development process or areas where additional training may be necessary. This analysis not only aids in refining the current project but also serves as a foundation for future projects, ensuring that the job portal continually evolves and improves. Establishing a culture of continuous improvement will ultimately enhance the reliability and user satisfaction of the job portal, which is crucial for its success within government agencies.

8 Launching the Job Portal

8.1 Preparing for Launch

Preparing for launch involves a multitude of critical steps that ensure the successful deployment of a job portal designed for government agencies. The first step is to conduct thorough testing of the platform. This includes functionality testing, user acceptance testing, and security assessments. Engaging a diverse group of stakeholders, such as potential users and technical staff, in these testing phases can uncover usability issues and ensure that the portal meets the specific needs of its target audience. It is essential to document all feedback and implement necessary changes before the official launch to enhance user experience.

Next, it is crucial to develop a comprehensive launch plan. This plan should detail the timeline of events leading up to the launch, including final testing phases, marketing strategies, and user training sessions. A successful launch plan incorporates communication strategies to inform stakeholders and potential users about the portal's features and benefits. Utilizing various channels such as email newsletters, social media, and webinars can effectively generate excitement and anticipation around the launch, ensuring a wider reach and engagement with the target audience.

Training is another vital component in preparing for launch. Government employees and users will need guidance on effectively navigating the job portal. Developing user manuals, instructional videos, and hosting training sessions can provide users with the necessary skills and confidence to utilize the platform. Additionally, having a dedicated support team ready to address queries and issues during the initial launch phase can significantly improve user satisfaction and minimize frustration.

Another key aspect of the launch preparation process is ensuring compliance with legal and regulatory requirements. Government agencies often operate under strict guidelines concerning data privacy, accessibility, and equal opportunity regulations. It is essential to conduct a final review to verify that the job portal adheres to all applicable laws and best practices. Collaborating with legal experts can provide assurance that the platform is not only functional but also compliant, thereby mitigating potential risks after the launch.

Finally, establishing metrics for success is crucial for assessing the effectiveness of the job portal post-launch. Defining key performance indicators (KPIs) such as user engagement rates, job application submissions, and feedback scores will help in measuring the portal's impact over time. Implementing analytics tools to track these metrics can provide valuable insights into user behavior and areas for improvement, paving the way for future enhancements. By preparing meticulously for launch, consultants can ensure that the job portal serves its intended purpose efficiently and effectively.

8.2 Marketing Strategies for Public Awareness

Marketing strategies for public awareness are essential in ensuring the successful launch and sustained engagement of a job portal designed for government agencies. A well-crafted marketing approach not only informs potential users about the platform but also builds trust and encourages them to utilize the services offered. As consultants involved in this project, understanding these strategies will enhance your ability to create a portal that meets its intended goals and reaches its target audience effectively.

To begin with, leveraging social media platforms is a crucial strategy for promoting public awareness. Given that social media is widely used by diverse demographics, creating targeted campaigns on platforms such as Facebook, Twitter, and LinkedIn can help reach a broad audience. Engaging content, such as informative posts about job opportunities, success stories from users, and updates on government initiatives, can stimulate interest and interaction. Regular posting and engagement with followers will foster a community around the job portal, increasing its visibility and appeal.

Another effective strategy is to collaborate with local government agencies and community organizations. By partnering with these entities, you can tap into existing networks and resources that can amplify your outreach efforts. Joint events, workshops, and informational sessions can be organized to demonstrate the features of the job portal and its benefits to potential users. These collaborations not only enhance credibility but also provide platforms for direct interaction with the community, allowing for immediate feedback and fostering a sense of ownership among users.

Content marketing is also vital in raising awareness about the job portal. Developing valuable and informative content, such as blogs, articles, and newsletters, can establish the portal as a trusted resource in the job-seeking landscape. Providing insights into the job market, career advice, and tips for navigating government employment processes can engage users and encourage them to return to the portal regularly. Utilizing search engine optimization (SEO) strategies will further increase the visibility of this content, ensuring that it reaches a wider audience actively searching for job-related information.

Email marketing can serve as a powerful tool for sustained engagement and awareness. Building a database of interested users and sending out regular updates about new job postings, features of the portal, and success stories can keep the audience informed and engaged. Personalized emails that address the specific needs of different user segments can enhance the effectiveness of this strategy. Additionally, encouraging users to share the portal with their networks can create a ripple effect, expanding the user base through word-of-mouth promotion.

In conclusion, implementing a multifaceted marketing strategy is essential for raising public awareness about a job portal for government agencies. By utilizing social media, collaborating with local organizations, engaging in content marketing, and leveraging email campaigns, consultants can create a robust framework that not only attracts users but also fosters a supportive community around the platform. These strategies will ultimately contribute to the portal's success, ensuring it becomes a vital resource for job seekers within the government sector.

8.3 Monitoring Initial Feedback

Monitoring initial feedback is a crucial phase in the development of a job portal for government agencies. This phase involves the systematic collection and analysis of user responses to the portal's features, functionalities, and overall user experience. Consultants must establish a robust feedback mechanism that allows users to share their thoughts and experiences as they navigate the portal. This can be achieved through surveys, focus groups, and direct interviews with users, ensuring a diverse range of perspectives is captured. By actively engaging with users, consultants can identify pain points and areas for improvement early in the process, which is vital to the portal's long-term success.

To effectively monitor feedback, consultants should implement a structured approach that categorizes responses into actionable insights. This can involve creating a framework that classifies feedback into various themes, such as usability, accessibility, and content relevance. By doing so, consultants can prioritize issues based on their frequency and impact. For instance, if multiple users express difficulty in navigating certain sections of the portal, this insight can lead to immediate adjustments in the user interface to enhance usability. This structured analysis not only streamlines the feedback process but also helps in documenting changes and improvements over time.

Additionally, leveraging technology can significantly enhance the feedback monitoring process. Consultants should consider utilizing analytics tools that track user behavior on the portal. Metrics such as time spent on pages, click-through rates, and drop-off points can provide quantitative data that complements qualitative feedback. This combination allows consultants to paint a fuller picture of user interactions and identify trends that may not be immediately evident through user comments alone. By integrating analytics into the feedback monitoring strategy, consultants can gain deeper insights into user engagement and satisfaction.

It is also essential for consultants to foster a culture of continuous improvement based on the feedback gathered. This involves not only addressing immediate concerns but also being proactive in anticipating future needs and expectations. Regularly updating stakeholders on feedback trends and proposed changes demonstrates a commitment to enhancing the user experience. This transparency can build trust among users and stakeholders alike, encouraging ongoing engagement with the portal. Furthermore, establishing a feedback loop where users see that their input leads to tangible changes can motivate them to continue providing insights.

Lastly, monitoring initial feedback should not be a one-time effort but rather an ongoing process. As the job portal evolves and more users engage with it, new feedback will emerge, necessitating continuous monitoring and adaptation. Consultants should schedule periodic reviews of feedback and performance data to ensure that the portal remains aligned with user needs and government objectives. By committing to this iterative process, consultants can help create a job portal that not only meets current requirements but also adapts to future challenges, ultimately leading to a more effective and user-friendly platform for government job seekers.

9 Post-Launch Support and Maintenance

9.1 Establishing Support Channels

Establishing support channels is a critical component in the successful deployment and management of a job portal for government agencies. A well-structured support system not only enhances user experience but also ensures that technical issues are resolved promptly, fostering trust and reliability among users. To create effective support channels, it is essential to identify the primary user groups, including job seekers, employers, and government personnel. Understanding their specific needs and challenges will help in designing tailored support services that address their concerns efficiently.

The first step in establishing support channels is to determine the most effective communication methods for each user group. Options may include a dedicated helpdesk, email support, live chat, and a comprehensive FAQ section. A helpdesk can serve as a central hub where inquiries are logged and tracked, allowing for organized responses and follow-ups. Live chat features can provide immediate assistance, catering to users who require urgent help. Meanwhile, a well-curated FAQ section can empower users to find answers to common questions independently, reducing the overall support workload.

Next, it is crucial to ensure that the support team is adequately trained and equipped with the necessary resources. This includes training on the technical aspects of the job portal, as well as understanding government policies and procedures relevant to employment services. Regular training sessions can be implemented to keep the team updated on new features, user feedback, and emerging issues. Moreover, providing the support team with access to a knowledge base will enable them to deliver accurate and timely information to users, enhancing overall service quality.

In addition to direct support channels, establishing a feedback mechanism is vital for continuous improvement. Encouraging users to provide feedback on their support experiences can reveal insights into common pain points and areas for enhancement. Surveys, suggestion boxes, and follow-up emails can be effective tools for gathering this information. Analyzing feedback data can inform adjustments in both the support processes and the job portal itself, ensuring the platform evolves in line with user needs and expectations.

Finally, promoting awareness of the available support channels among users is essential for maximizing their effectiveness. This can be achieved through onboarding sessions, informational webinars, and user guides that outline how to access support resources. Regular updates via newsletters or notifications about new support features or resources can keep users informed and engaged. By establishing robust support channels and actively promoting them, government agencies can significantly improve user satisfaction and ensure the job portal remains a valuable resource for all stakeholders involved.

9.2 Regular Maintenance and Updates

Regular maintenance and updates are critical to the longevity and effectiveness of a job portal designed for government agencies. Once the portal is launched, the initial excitement can fade, but it is essential to recognize that ongoing support is necessary to ensure the system operates smoothly. Regular maintenance involves routine checks and updates to the software, hardware, and security protocols that underpin the job portal. This proactive approach helps identify potential issues before they escalate into significant problems, thus maintaining the portal's reliability and efficiency.

One of the fundamental aspects of maintenance is ensuring that the software remains up to date. This includes applying patches and updates released by the software providers to fix bugs, enhance functionality, and improve security. Government job portals often handle sensitive information, and outdated software can expose these systems to security vulnerabilities. Additionally, keeping the software current ensures compatibility with new technologies and features that can improve the user experience, making it easier for job seekers and agencies to navigate the portal.

In parallel with software updates, regular content maintenance is crucial. Job postings, resources, and informational articles must be current and relevant. Outdated job listings can frustrate users and lead to a loss of trust in the portal's reliability. Establishing a routine for content review and updates not only keeps the information fresh but also enhances the portal's SEO performance, making it more visible to job seekers. Furthermore, integrating feedback from users can guide content adjustments and introduce new sections that cater to the evolving needs of both job seekers and employers.

Security updates are another critical component of regular maintenance. As cyber threats evolve, safeguarding user data becomes increasingly important, especially for government agencies that handle sensitive information. Implementing regular security audits, vulnerability assessments, and penetration testing can help identify weaknesses in the system. Additionally, educating staff and users about cybersecurity best practices can reduce the risk of breaches and foster a culture of security awareness within the organization.

Ultimately, establishing a maintenance and update schedule is essential for the sustainability of a government job portal. This framework should outline responsibilities, timelines, and processes for conducting maintenance activities. By prioritizing regular maintenance and updates, consultants can ensure that the job portal not only meets the current needs of its users but also adapts to future changes in technology, user expectations, and governmental regulations. This commitment to ongoing improvement will enhance the portal's reputation and effectiveness, contributing to a successful job search experience for all stakeholders involved.

9.3 Gathering User Feedback for Improvements

Gathering user feedback is a critical component in the development and enhancement of a job portal for government agencies. It serves as a bridge between user needs and the functionalities offered by the portal. To create a user-centric platform, consultants must prioritize collecting feedback from various stakeholders, including job seekers, employers, and agency personnel. By understanding their experiences, challenges, and suggestions, consultants can make informed decisions that lead to continuous improvements, ensuring the portal effectively meets its objectives.

The first step in gathering user feedback is to identify the target audience and the best methods for reaching them. Surveys and questionnaires are often effective tools for collecting quantitative data, as they can be distributed widely and analyzed for trends. However, qualitative feedback is equally important, and this can be obtained through interviews and focus groups. These methods allow for deeper insights into user experiences and can reveal issues that may not be immediately apparent through numerical data alone. Ensuring that feedback mechanisms are accessible and user-friendly is essential to maximize participation and obtain meaningful insights.

Once feedback is collected, it is crucial to analyze the data systematically. This process involves categorizing feedback into themes and identifying common pain points shared by users. Consultants should pay attention to both positive feedback and constructive criticism. Positive feedback can highlight features that are working well and should be maintained, while constructive criticism can pinpoint areas for improvement. Utilizing data analysis tools can streamline this process and help visualize trends over time, enabling consultants to track changes and progress in user satisfaction.

Following the analysis, consultants should engage in iterative development, where user feedback directly informs the next stages of the portal's design and functionality. This approach allows for rapid prototyping and testing of new features based on user suggestions. It is important to communicate any changes made as a result of feedback back to the users, fostering a sense of community and partnership. This transparency not only builds trust but also encourages ongoing feedback, creating a cycle of continuous improvement.

Finally, establishing a culture of feedback within the organization is vital for long-term success. Consultants should advocate for regular feedback sessions and make user feedback an integral part of the portal's development lifecycle. Creating a dedicated feedback channel, such as a forum or suggestion box, can keep the lines of communication open. By institutionalizing feedback mechanisms, government agencies can ensure that their job portal evolves in line with user needs, ultimately leading to a more effective and user-friendly platform that serves its intended purpose.

10 Measuring Success

10.1 Key Performance Indicators (KPIs)

Key Performance Indicators (KPIs) are essential metrics that help assess the effectiveness and success of a job portal specifically designed for government agencies. These indicators provide valuable insights into how well the platform is performing in relation to its objectives. By establishing clear KPIs, consultants can track progress, identify areas for improvement, and ensure that the portal meets the needs of both job seekers and government employers. This subchapter will explore the various KPIs that should be considered when building a job portal for a government organization.

One of the most critical KPIs to monitor is the number of job postings on the portal. This metric reflects the level of engagement from government agencies and their willingness to utilize the platform for recruitment. A steady or increasing number of job postings indicates that the portal is gaining traction among agencies, while a decline may signal the need for additional outreach or support. Consultants should analyze trends in job postings over time to assess whether specific interventions or marketing strategies are effective in attracting more agencies to the platform.

Another vital KPI is the user engagement rate, which measures how actively job seekers interact with the portal. This can include metrics such as the number of registered users, the frequency of visits, and the average duration of each session. High user engagement is often indicative of a user-friendly interface and valuable content, while low engagement may necessitate improvements in the user experience or the types of job listings available. Consultants should employ tools like heatmaps and user feedback surveys to gain deeper insights into user behavior and preferences.

Conversion rates are another key performance indicator that consultants should focus on. This metric tracks the percentage of users who take specific actions, such as applying for a job or creating a profile. A high conversion rate suggests that the portal is effectively facilitating the job application process, while a low rate may point to obstacles in the user journey, such as complicated application forms or unclear instructions. Analyzing conversion rates can help consultants identify specific areas of the application process that require refinement to enhance user satisfaction and increase successful placements.

Lastly, the time-to-hire metric is crucial for evaluating the efficiency of the job portal. This KPI measures the duration from when a job is posted to when a candidate is hired. A shorter time-to-hire indicates that the portal is successfully connecting employers with suitable candidates quickly. Conversely, a longer time-to-hire may reveal bottlenecks in the recruitment process or suggest that the portal is not attracting the right talent. By monitoring this KPI, consultants can work with government agencies to streamline hiring processes and improve the overall effectiveness of the job portal.

In conclusion, establishing and monitoring KPIs is fundamental to the success of a job portal tailored for government agencies. By focusing on metrics such as job postings, user engagement, conversion rates, and time-to-hire, consultants can gain critical insights into the portal's performance. These indicators not only help in assessing the platform's effectiveness but also guide ongoing improvements to ensure it meets the needs of both job seekers and government employers. Ultimately, a data-driven approach to KPIs will lead to a more successful and impactful job portal.

10.2 Analyzing User Engagement

Analyzing user engagement is a critical component in the development and ongoing success of a job portal for government agencies. Understanding how users interact with the platform provides insights into their needs, preferences, and pain points. This analysis allows consultants to make informed decisions that enhance user experience, increase efficiency, and ultimately lead to higher job placement rates. By employing various analytical tools and techniques, consultants can gather quantitative and qualitative data on user behavior, which informs the design and functionality of the portal.

One of the primary metrics for assessing user engagement is the user retention rate. This metric indicates how many users return to the portal after their initial visit. A high retention rate suggests that users find value in the portal's offerings, while a low rate may signal issues with user experience or content relevance. By analyzing the pathways users take through the portal, consultants can identify which features keep users engaged and which may need re-evaluation. This information can guide future enhancements, ensuring that the portal evolves in alignment with user expectations.

Moreover, tracking user interactions with various features of the job portal is essential for understanding engagement levels. Metrics such as click-through rates on job postings, the frequency of application submissions, and the use of additional resources like resume-building tools or interview preparation materials provide a comprehensive picture of user engagement. Understanding which areas of the portal are most frequently accessed can help identify successful elements of the design, while less popular features may require further investigation or redesign to improve usability.

User feedback is another crucial aspect of engagement analysis. Surveys, interviews, and focus groups can provide qualitative insights that quantitative data may overlook. Engaging with users directly allows consultants to gather their thoughts on the portal's functionality and design, uncovering hidden barriers to engagement. This feedback can also guide the development of user personas, which represent the diverse needs and preferences of the portal's audience. Tailoring the user experience based on these personas ensures that the portal meets the unique demands of its users.

Finally, it is vital to utilize analytics tools to continuously monitor user engagement over time. This ongoing analysis not only helps in assessing the immediate impact of changes made to the portal but also provides a framework for long-term strategy development. By setting key performance indicators (KPIs) and regularly reviewing these metrics, consultants can adapt to shifts in user behavior and expectations. This proactive approach ensures that the job portal remains relevant and effective in fulfilling its mission of connecting job seekers with government employment opportunities.

10.3 Reporting and Continuous Improvement

Reporting and continuous improvement are essential components in the lifecycle of a job portal for government agencies. Establishing a robust reporting framework enables stakeholders to track the performance of the portal and gauge its effectiveness in meeting objectives. Regular reporting should include metrics such as user engagement, job postings, application rates, and user satisfaction. By analyzing these key performance indicators (KPIs), consultants can ensure that the portal aligns with the needs of both job seekers and employers while fulfilling the government's employment objectives.

To facilitate effective reporting, it's crucial to implement a user-friendly dashboard that aggregates data from various sources. This dashboard should not only present real-time statistics but also allow for historical comparisons to identify trends over time. A comprehensive reporting system should encompass both quantitative and qualitative data, enabling a deeper understanding of user experiences. Incorporating feedback mechanisms, such as surveys or focus groups, will provide deeper insights into user satisfaction and reveal areas requiring attention. This holistic approach helps create a more responsive and user-centered job portal.

Continuous improvement hinges on the analysis of the data collected through the reporting process. Consultants should adopt a proactive mindset, utilizing insights gained from user interaction with the portal to inform iterative enhancements. This might involve refining the user interface, optimizing search functionalities, or diversifying job categories based on emerging employment trends. Regularly scheduled assessments can also facilitate the identification of any barriers that users encounter, allowing for timely interventions that enhance the overall user experience.

Moreover, fostering a culture of continuous improvement necessitates collaboration among stakeholders. Engaging government representatives, end-users, and technical teams in the improvement process ensures that diverse perspectives are considered. Regular workshops or feedback sessions can serve as platforms for discussing findings from the reporting phase and brainstorming potential solutions. This collaborative approach not only strengthens relationships among stakeholders but also enhances the overall effectiveness of the job portal by ensuring it remains adaptable to changing needs.

In conclusion, the reporting and continuous improvement processes are critical for the long-term success of a job portal for government agencies. By establishing a strong reporting framework and committing to ongoing enhancements based on data-driven insights, consultants can help create a portal that not only meets the immediate needs of users but also evolves in response to future challenges and opportunities. This commitment to continuous improvement will ultimately lead to a more effective job portal that supports the strategic goals of government employment initiatives.

11 Case Studies and Best Practices

11.1 Successful Job Portals in Government

Successful job portals in government leverage technology to streamline the recruitment process, enhancing efficiency and accessibility for both job seekers and employers. These platforms are designed to connect qualified candidates with various government positions, ensuring that the hiring process is transparent and equitable. By adopting best practices from successful government job portals, consultants can create systems that not only meet the unique needs of government agencies but also improve overall public service delivery.

One prominent example of a successful government job portal is USAJOBS, which serves as the federal government's official employment site. This platform effectively aggregates job listings from various federal agencies, offering a user-friendly interface that allows candidates to search for opportunities based on location, job type, and agency. The success of USAJOBS can be attributed to its commitment to user experience, providing comprehensive resources such as application tips, resume writing guides, and information on the federal hiring process. Consultants should take note of the importance of a well-organized and informative portal structure to enhance user engagement and satisfaction.

Another notable instance is the UK's Civil Service Jobs portal, which focuses on attracting diverse talent to public service roles. This platform emphasizes inclusivity and accessibility, offering features such as easy navigation for individuals with disabilities and multilingual support. By incorporating these elements, the Civil Service Jobs portal not only fulfills legal obligations but also broadens the talent pool from which government agencies can draw. Consultants can learn from this approach by integrating accessibility tools and inclusive practices into their job portal designs to better serve all potential candidates.

Additionally, the State of California's CalCareers platform exemplifies how data analytics can enhance recruitment efforts. CalCareers utilizes analytics to track user behavior, helping to identify trends in candidate applications and agency hiring patterns. This data-driven approach enables government agencies to make informed decisions about their recruitment strategies and refine their outreach efforts. For consultants, incorporating analytics into the job portal development process can lead to more effective marketing campaigns and targeted recruitment initiatives, ultimately resulting in a stronger workforce.

Finally, the success of government job portals is often tied to their ability to provide ongoing support and resources to both job seekers and employers. Portals that offer career counseling, webinars, and workshops create a supportive environment that fosters career development. By collaborating with local educational institutions and professional organizations, consultants can enhance the value of their portals, ensuring that they not only serve as job listing sites but also as comprehensive career development platforms. This holistic approach can lead to a more engaged workforce and improved public service outcomes.

11.2 Lessons Learned from Failed Projects

Failed projects in the realm of job portals for government agencies can provide valuable insights for consultants aiming to achieve success in future initiatives. One of the primary lessons learned is the importance of understanding the specific needs and requirements of the target audience. Many failed projects stem from a lack of comprehensive research and engagement with stakeholders, resulting in a platform that does not meet the users' expectations. Consultants must prioritize thorough needs assessments, including interviews and surveys with potential users, to develop a job portal that addresses their unique challenges and preferences.

Another critical lesson is the necessity of clear communication and collaboration among all project stakeholders. Failed projects often reflect poor alignment between government agencies, technology vendors, and end-users. This misalignment can lead to misunderstandings regarding project goals, timelines, and deliverables. Establishing regular communication channels and collaborative frameworks can help ensure that all parties are on the same page throughout the project lifecycle. By fostering a culture of transparency and teamwork, consultants can mitigate the risks of miscommunication and enhance project outcomes.

Additionally, the significance of adaptability in project management cannot be overstated. Many failed projects struggle due to rigid adherence to initial plans, even when changing circumstances warrant adjustments. Effective consultants recognize the importance of being agile and responsive to new information, user feedback, and technological advancements. Incorporating iterative development practices, such as agile methodologies, can enable teams to make necessary adjustments and improvements in real-time, ultimately leading to a more successful job portal.

Budget management is another area where many projects falter. Insufficient financial planning or unexpected costs can derail a project, leading to incomplete features or delays. Successful consultants understand the importance of creating a realistic budget that includes contingencies for unforeseen expenses. This approach not only ensures that the project remains financially viable but also allows for the inclusion of essential features that enhance the user experience. Regular financial reviews throughout the project can help identify potential issues early, enabling proactive adjustments.

Finally, the significance of post-launch evaluation cannot be overlooked. Many failed projects do not incorporate a robust plan for assessing the effectiveness of the job portal after its launch. Continuous monitoring and evaluation help identify areas for improvement and ensure that the platform evolves to meet changing user needs. Consultants should advocate for establishing key performance indicators (KPIs) and feedback mechanisms that facilitate ongoing assessment. By learning from both successes and failures, consultants can refine their approaches and contribute to the development of more effective job portals for government agencies.

11.3 Best Practices for Future Projects

When embarking on the development of a job portal for government agencies, adopting best practices can significantly enhance the project's success. First and foremost, it is crucial to conduct comprehensive stakeholder analysis. Engaging with all relevant stakeholders, including government officials, job seekers, employers, and IT professionals, ensures that the portal meets the diverse needs of its users. Gathering input through interviews, surveys, and focus groups provides valuable insights into the features and functionalities required in the portal. This foundational step sets the stage for creating a user-centric platform that aligns with the goals of the agency and the expectations of its users.

Effective project management methodologies are another cornerstone of success. Utilizing agile project management can facilitate flexibility and adaptability throughout the development process. By breaking the project into manageable sprints, teams can focus on delivering incremental improvements while remaining responsive to feedback. Regular check-ins and updates help to keep all stakeholders informed and engaged, fostering a collaborative environment that encourages innovation. Additionally, maintaining a clear timeline with defined milestones ensures that the project stays on track and within budget, allowing for timely adjustments as necessary.

Incorporating robust testing and quality assurance practices is essential to ensure the portal's reliability and user satisfaction. A thorough testing phase should include functional testing, usability testing, and performance testing to identify and resolve any issues before the portal goes live. Engaging real users during the testing process provides critical feedback on the portal's usability and functionality. Addressing any identified shortcomings early on not only enhances the user experience but also builds trust in the system, which is particularly important for government platforms.

Post-launch support and continuous improvement are vital for the long-term success of the job portal. Establishing a feedback mechanism to gather user experiences and suggestions allows for ongoing enhancements to the platform. Regular updates and maintenance are necessary to address any technical issues and to incorporate new features based on user needs and technological advancements. Furthermore, training sessions and resources for users can significantly increase adoption rates and ensure that the portal is utilized effectively by all stakeholders.

Finally, ensuring compliance with legal and regulatory requirements cannot be overlooked when creating a job portal for government agencies. It is essential to stay informed about privacy laws, accessibility standards, and employment regulations that may affect the portal's design and functionality. Collaborating with legal experts throughout the development process can help mitigate risks associated with non-compliance. By integrating best practices in compliance from the outset, consultants can deliver a job portal that not only serves its purpose effectively but also upholds the standards expected of government services.

12 Conclusion and Future Trends

12.1 Recap of Key Takeaways

The development of a job portal for government agencies involves a series of critical steps that ensure the platform meets the unique needs of both employers and job seekers. One of the primary takeaways is the importance of conducting a comprehensive needs assessment before any technical development begins. This involves engaging with stakeholders, including government officials, HR representatives, and potential users, to gather insights about their requirements, preferences, and expectations.

Understanding the specific challenges faced by government agencies in recruitment is essential to tailor the portal's functionalities accordingly.

Another key takeaway is the significance of user-centered design throughout the development process. The portal must be intuitive and accessible, accommodating users with varying levels of technological proficiency. Implementing usability testing at various stages allows for the identification of pain points, ensuring that the final product is user-friendly. This approach not only enhances the user experience but also increases the likelihood of widespread adoption among both job seekers and employers within government agencies.

Data security and compliance are paramount in the creation of a job portal for government use. Consultants must be well-versed in relevant regulations, such as data protection laws and accessibility standards, to ensure that the portal adheres to legal requirements. Building robust security measures into the portal design helps protect sensitive information and fosters trust among users. Establishing clear data governance policies is also essential to manage user data responsibly and maintain the integrity of the recruitment process.

The integration of advanced technologies, such as artificial intelligence and machine learning, can significantly enhance the functionality of the job portal. These technologies can streamline the recruitment process by automating resume screening, matching candidates with suitable job openings, and providing analytics to improve hiring practices. Consultants should advocate for the incorporation of such features while remaining mindful of the need for transparency and fairness in algorithmic decision-making.

Finally, continuous evaluation and improvement are indispensable for the long-term success of a government job portal. After launch, it is vital to gather feedback from users and stakeholders to assess the portal's performance and identify areas for enhancement. Establishing a feedback loop enables ongoing adjustments and upgrades, ensuring that the portal evolves with changing technology and user needs. By focusing on these key takeaways, consultants can effectively guide government agencies in creating a job portal that not only meets current demands but also adapts to future challenges in the recruitment landscape.

12.2 The Future of Job Portals in Government

The future of job portals in government is poised for significant transformation, driven by advancements in technology and changing workforce expectations. As governments increasingly recognize the importance of attracting top talent, job portals will evolve to become more user-friendly, efficient, and integrated with other governmental processes. This evolution will not only enhance the experience for job seekers but will also streamline recruitment processes for agencies. By leveraging data analytics, artificial intelligence, and machine learning, government job portals can provide tailored job recommendations, predictive hiring analytics, and real-time insights into labor market trends.

One of the most promising developments in the future of government job portals is the integration of artificial intelligence. AI can help automate various aspects of the recruitment process, from resume screening to candidate engagement. This technology will enable agencies to quickly identify the most qualified candidates, thereby reducing the time and resources spent on manual evaluations. Furthermore, AI-driven chatbots can enhance user experience by providing real-time assistance to applicants, answering their queries, and guiding them through the application process. This integration not only improves efficiency but also fosters a more inclusive and accessible hiring process.

Data security and privacy will play a crucial role in shaping the future of job portals within government organizations. As these platforms collect and process large amounts of personal data, it is essential to implement robust security measures to protect sensitive information. Compliance with regulations such as GDPR and ensuring user trust will be paramount. Future job portals will need to incorporate advanced encryption methods and secure authentication protocols to safeguard user data. Additionally, transparency in how data is used will be vital for maintaining public trust and ensuring that applicants feel safe in sharing their information.

Collaboration among various government agencies will also redefine the landscape of job portals. By creating a centralized job portal that aggregates opportunities across different departments, applicants will have a more comprehensive view of available positions. This centralized approach not only simplifies the job search process for applicants but also allows government agencies to share best practices, resources, and insights about effective recruitment strategies. Future job portals may also facilitate cross-agency collaborations, enabling the pooling of talent and resources to address workforce shortages in critical areas.

Finally, the user experience will become a central focus in the design and functionality of government job portals. As job seekers increasingly expect seamless and intuitive online experiences, job portals will need to prioritize usability and accessibility. This may involve redesigning interfaces, optimizing for mobile devices, and ensuring compliance with accessibility standards for individuals with disabilities. By focusing on user experience, government job portals can enhance engagement and encourage more applicants to explore career opportunities within the public sector, ultimately leading to a more diverse and capable workforce that meets the needs of the community.

12.3 Final Thoughts and Next Steps

As you reach the conclusion of this journey through the process of creating a job portal for government agencies, it is essential to reflect on the key takeaways and the critical components of a successful implementation. The landscape of government recruitment is continuously evolving, and a well-crafted job portal is central to streamlining this process. The insights discussed throughout this book serve as a blueprint to guide consultants in effectively addressing the unique needs of government agencies, ensuring that the final product is not only functional but also user-friendly and inclusive.

The initial phase of developing a job portal requires thorough research and analysis. Understanding the specific requirements of the government organization, including compliance with regulations, accessibility standards, and integration with existing systems, is paramount. Engaging with stakeholders early in the process helps to identify pain points and desired features, which will inform the design and functionality of the portal. This collaborative approach fosters a sense of ownership among stakeholders and ensures that the portal aligns with the broader objectives of the agency.

Once the foundational requirements are established, the next step is to focus on the user experience. A job portal must cater to a diverse audience, including job seekers, human resource personnel, and hiring managers. Streamlined navigation, clear job descriptions, and comprehensive search functionalities are essential elements that enhance user engagement. Additionally, incorporating features like mobile responsiveness and multilingual support can significantly broaden access, ensuring that the portal serves all segments of the community effectively.

After the design and development phases, the emphasis should shift toward testing and deployment. Rigorous testing processes, including user acceptance testing, help identify any issues before going live. Training sessions for agency staff and ongoing support will facilitate a smooth transition to the new system. Post-launch, it is vital to monitor the portal's performance and gather user feedback to make iterative improvements. This commitment to continuous enhancement reflects a dedication to service excellence and responsiveness to user needs.

In closing, the journey of creating a job portal for government agencies is both challenging and rewarding. As consultants, your role is crucial in navigating this complex landscape, ensuring that the final product not only meets technical specifications but also serves the community effectively. By staying informed about emerging trends and technologies in recruitment, and by maintaining open lines of communication with stakeholders, you can position yourself as a valuable partner in the ongoing development of government recruitment processes. Embrace the final thoughts shared in this book as a call to action, encouraging you to take the next steps in your consultancy journey with confidence and clarity.